Sisters & Courtesans

ISBN 13:978-0615983141

Cover: Peter A. Duval

Kelsay Books
White Violet Press
24600 Mountain Avenue 35
Hemet, California 92544

Sisters & Courtesans

Anna M. Evans

Kelsay Books

Contents

My Life as a Vestal Virgin

It smells of earth inside this tiny room
beneath the ground. The guards have sealed it up.
A tallow candle gutters in the gloom,
illuminates the single bowl, the cup.
I couldn't know, when as a girl of eight
I was delivered to the sacred fire,
what torture lay before me in this fate,
a woman, bound by rules, ruled by desire.
I fought the way my blood sang with the need,
but when he kissed me, something wild and sly
uncurled within me, desperate to be freed.
Yes, I still want him, even as I die.
I broke my vow and yet the hearth stayed lit.
Whatever insults Rome, men bury it.

My Life as an Ambitious Former Greek Porne

Born a slave, at thirteen I was sold
to a pimp who auctioned my virginity—
two minas. Since that day I've seen untold
numbers of men. And now, at last, I'm free!
But what am I supposed to do? No man
is going to marry someone with my past.
I'm working on the streets, but with a plan:
my tutor says I'm clever and learn fast.
And I'm still pretty. With an education,
who knows what kind of clients I'll attract?
Those, I hope, who like good conversation
with one who's learned philosophy and tact.
I am a diligent and supple girl,
born to prosper in this modern world.

My Life as a Docta Puella

A poet is in love with me. He writes
about my soft skin and my silken hair
then rages that I spend so many nights
with other men. It's sweet of him to care.
He's handsome, young, and pretty good in bed
plus I like hearing him declaim his verse,
but poetry, alas, won't buy me bread
or put *denarii* inside my purse.
I have to ply my trade with rich old men
who paw me and have problems getting hard,
and when I'm with my poet once again
he's sulky as a child and on his guard.
I wish he were a wealthy entrepreneur.
I didn't study Plato to stay poor.

My Life as the Woman at the Well

I always went for water when the sun
was at its height—I didn't want to see
the other township women, who would shun
my friendship while they whispered next to me.
I had outlived five husbands; when the last
one died no one would marry me for fear,
but Jesus didn't care about my past,
my origins. He simply said, *Come here*,
and asked for water. I drew Him a cup,
and then He told me Lord God had forgiven
all my sins, that I would be drawn up—
if I believed and lived well—into heaven.
Though I'm not sure if all of that is true,
at least I get respect now, which will do.

My Life as a Han Dynasty Concubine

The Emperor has hundreds just like me,
sent here as tributes, bribes, or just because
a daughter's worth so little by our laws.
I doubt if I will ever get to see
the room of His Imperial Majesty
and that's just fine. My daily household chores
are light. And I've discovered where the key
hangs that unlocks the palace library.
I've taught myself to read behind closed doors.
While other consorts jockey for his time,
and press their portraits in his eunuch's hand,
I'm busy learning how to write in rhyme.
No one, of course, will ever read a word,
and that's just fine. It's better in this land
to speak out only if you can't be heard.

My Life as a Druidess

I stir the steaming entrails on the ground
with my oak stick. The pattern that resolves
is just a frame to hang my words around.

The subtle art of prophecy involves
seeing what the king wants to come true,
so the restraint that holds him back dissolves.

I listen, scheme, and figure the long view—
the Romans gone, the Celtic people whole—
and set the course we need to get us through.

A little theater's all it takes. I roll
my eyes back, mumble, wail. He doesn't guess
how much the kingdom's under my control

or if he does, he's wise enough to bless
the greater wisdom of his druidess.

My Life as the May Queen of Beltane

I led the cows between the sacred fires,
wearing a crown of willow on my head
and bearing an ash wand. That night, desires
hung in the air like a mist of things unsaid.
Couples crept off to ditch or barn or lea.
I sat in state with Brendan, my Green Man
until he turned and, leaning over me,
held out his hand. Of one accord we ran
over the hills until we found a cave,
where we lay down and satisfied the rite—
maid though I was, I took more than I gave.
I won't forget him or that holy night,
not least because this child now at my breast,
born of a Beltane union, is thrice blessed.

My Life as a Temple Prostitute

I think I'm fifteen now. It's been four years
since Father brought me sobbing here one dawn
and begged me to stop shaming him with tears.

I married the God out on the temple lawn,
and then began my duties. I don't know
why pilgrims spilling seed in me is prayer.

The men who come here never seem to show
much holy grace—they don't pretend to care
about the shrine, the statue made of gold.

Slow days, I polish Him from head to toe.
I dust His ruby lips, and try to hold
the fingers of his outstretched hand, as though

He were my husband, proud of His young wife.
Sometimes it almost feels like normal life.

My Life as an Anglo-Saxon Novitiate

I was quite lonely here at first. Each day
Vespers took a long time coming round.
I missed our dog, but then, in lieu of pay
the Abbess got a German hunting hound
and I was singled out to be her keeper.
Hilda, as they named her, has bright eyes
that take in everything. I swear she's deeper
than most people I meet. Now, when I rise
at Prime she waits for me with wagging tail.
I feed her scraps and then on our long walk
she catches rabbits, hares, and once a quail.
I know it's silent time, but still I talk
to her. I think we're part of God's great plan—
we can't know how, just do the best we can.

My Life as a Norse Spae-Wife

It is a woman's work to spin the wool
and hum the secret hexes that embed
the spell in every fiber of the spool.
The next skill is to take the skein of thread
and weave the banner as you chant the charms
that bind the battle emblem to the cloth.
So when the men amass and take up arms,
the raven standard rises up aloft.

Alas, I made the flag that Ubbe flew
at Cynwit, which was captured by the thanes.
They say I'm a weak witch. This may be true,
better than own it's possible our Danes
made a mistake, that magic is absurd—
the banner, just a picture of a bird.

My Life as a Serving Wench of the Round Table

Everyone seems to think those knights were sainted.
I have to say I didn't see much sign
and I was, how to put it, well-acquainted,
with quite a few of them. I served their wine.
After a jug or two they would get loud
and try to feel me up. Gawain was cute—
I let him have me right before he vowed
off women. Gareth acted like a brute
and tried to force me once but I got clear.
Percival was kinky, so was Kay.
Lancelot would call me Guinevere.
I did love Galahad, but he was gay.
King Arthur, though a noble man and kind,
was, to all their faults, completely blind.

My Life in the Third Crusade

Hearing the papal call I was inspired
to join King Richard's army at the rear.
The women's sub-division was required

to cook and wash, and polish knightly gear,
to sharpen weapons, carry ammunition,
and scout ahead to check that all was clear,

which all seemed suited to our weak condition.
But at the siege of Acre we joined the fight—
ordered up front, we heard it was our mission

to fill the city's moats before first light.
We formed a chain, passed pails of rock and wood
to get it done. We labored thus all night

and made the ground on which our siege-towers stood
to bring death to the city. God is good.

My Life as Genghis Khan's Morganatic Wife

Some nights he would have nightmares and awake
all drenched in sweat. I dared not ask him why,
and so I'd just distract him, aim to make
him laugh or turn him on. He was quite shy
in bed—I always tried to drive him crazy,
yet he preferred to lie there, let me do
the work. In truth, he was a little lazy,
or tired perhaps. He always looked worn through.
Of course, he'd leave for months, off on campaign
and I would mope around the palace, bored,
wishing I were on horseback on the plain,
a crack shot archer with the Golden Horde,
but I was just a girl. Some nights, he'd weep,
and after sex I'd sing him back to sleep.

My Life as Joan of Arc's Maidservant

She didn't like me fussing, wouldn't let
me draw her bath or brush her short brown hair.
She wanted me to kneel by her in prayer
then play a game of chess with her. She'd set
out pieces carved in ivory and jet,
but leave off both her knights, which made it fair.
I lost more times than not but didn't care.
She was the most amazing girl I'd met,
so chaste and pure. We wouldn't ever touch
except before a battle. Then I went
to bring her armor to her private tent,
helped her buckle it on, the breastplate last.
My fingers grazed her neck each time they passed,
and I said nothing because I felt too much.

My Life as a Camp Follower

The fight keeps dragging on. My soldier lover
was badly wounded by a Yorkist axe.
I came here in the hope that he'd recover,
and stayed on after, in the army's tracks.
It's easy living—all the men are lonely
and most are gentle. I say I'm a nurse
although I tend to them in one way only
and then I slip their pennies in my purse.
I use a pessary of wool and wine
and drink mint tea in secret. If they saw
they'd call it witchcraft. Well, the risk is mine,
all part of women's lot. The men make war
and corpses pile crotch deep in England's mud.
So many things in life come down to blood.

My Life as an Aztec Sacrifice

I am the Goddess. Slaves caress my feet,
feed me avocadoes from their hands,
drape me in purple cloth. The wine is sweet.
I sway a little on the ritual sands.
People adore me, touch my skin and hair,
push golden bangles onto both my wrists.
A murmur rises, gentle as a prayer.
I don't want more to drink but the boy insists.
This is my moment, never will I feel
as loved, as worshipped, as I do tonight.
Here on the platform, nothing seems quite real
except the moon, which shines with eerie light.
I am still breathing as the people start
to cheer the priest who lifts my burning heart.

My Life as a Tudor Abbess

Thank God we have the Queen now. All is well—
my nuns and I are camping in the abbey
though half the roof is gone, the nave's a shell,
and both the transepts look a little shabby.
Still, we are back, and slowly can rebuild
the things that monster, Henry, tried to raze.
Meanwhile we pray for all the blood he spilled,
and for the soon return of better days.

Daily, I lead a prayer for our new Queen,
that she may find the power to forgive
the Protestants for everything we've seen,
that she may let her young half-sister live,
and that the girl embrace Catholicism.
Too many have died already in this schism.

My Life as an Honest Courtesan in Venice

I must confess that I can barely walk
in these new shoes, the platforms are so high.
Advancing regally, I pause to talk

(and rest) when an acquaintance passes by.
These split brocaded sleeves force me to hold
my arms spread out as if I mean to fly.

My heavy pendant heart is solid gold.
I hope it's the epitome of class—
for that's the point of all this, so I'm told.

I may be *nouveau riche*, but I can pass.
Don't ever dare to lump me in with whores
with their thin skirts and ornaments of brass.

And as for those new sumptuary laws
I am exempted by a special clause.

My Life as One of King Charles II's Mistresses

There is a portrait of me—I look pretty,
perhaps a little too much skin on show,
but Peter Lely captured me, a glow
I had when nineteen, mischievous and witty.
I could have had my pick of the whole city,
but then, the king was quite the man, you know.
And for the seven months he was my beau
I was content. Indeed, it was a pity
my husband found us out, and sent me down
to his estate a hundred miles from town.
But, silver linings! When the black plague struck
I wasn't there. Nor was I, with more luck,
when our fine mansion burned down to the ground.
My husband's corpse, alas, was never found.

My Life as a Sworn Virgin of Albania

Most people think I did it to escape
my marriage contract. He was old and mean
and sex would have been tantamount to rape

but that's not really why. Thing is, I'd seen
my sister marry, bear three kids then die
a virtual prisoner, and I wasn't keen

to live that life. No, I preferred to try
alcohol and cigarettes, to play
guitar and gamble, even fight, if I

so chose. Of course, the other women say
I'm missing out on what men bring to bed.
Frankly, I'd take my right hand any day.

My sex life may be locked up in my head
but I will be a free man till I'm dead.

My Life as a "First Fleeter"

I wasn't sure if I should laugh or wail
when the Judge said, "Transportation." We all knew
that still meant death or worse. The fleet set sail
in fine May weather. Soon enough the crew
were looking for the pretty girls to screw.
I caught a break and turned the surgeon's head.
His quarters were just big enough for two.
He was all right—I knew we couldn't wed
but I was safe from bother in his bed.
Eight months at sea, then into Botany Bay.
Of course it was a while since I'd last bled—
and so I knew a child was on the way.
He'll be as bright as brass and tough as nails,
the firstborn citizen of New South Wales.

My Life as a French Carmelite Nun

Outside these walls the revolution rages,
but inside all is calm and I am safe,
tending the garden—tomatoes in their cages,
the vegetable patch. When restrictions chafe
I climb up to the highest tower and view
the city burning, riots in the square.
It's true there's often not that much to do,
but better cloistered here than dead out there.
In my hours of silent contemplation
I must confess I've wondered about God,
his tolerance for death and desecration.
Then yesterday I saw a sign, a clod
of earth that looked like Jesus. Vive la France!
It's good to know that nothing's left to chance.

My Life as a Russian Orthodox Nun

My grand duchess took orders well before
the trouble started. I was glad to go
with Europe heading for a bloody war.

And then the revolution struck. The snow
was knee deep on the night they came for us—
she was an aristocrat, I guess, although

she'd sold her jewels to help the poor, owned less
than anyone. They held us in a school,
then gave us to the *cheka*. I confess

I was afraid. But my lady kept her cool
even as they threw us down, tossed in
the hand grenades. She said, *The golden rule*

is: don't let the bastards have a single thing.
She squeezed my hand and then began to sing.

My Life as a Geisha

At first I loved the pomp and elegance—
elaborate make up, hairstyles, fancy dress.
My favorite was to have men watch me dance
(and size up their erections, I confess.)
But soon, it all got old, the endless tea,
the small talk that was always about them.
I wanted to scream, *Come on, look at me!*
Aren't I supposed to be a priceless gem?
One evening an old client brought a man
from Europe to the teahouse. Eyes as bright
as summer skies! He asked how I began
my Geisha training, and we talked all night.
I really thought he liked me, then the clown
begged me to strip naked and lie down.

My Life as a Nineteenth Century Trance Lecturer

Ask me a question and I'll answer it,
convince you I'm communing with the dead.
A silly girl like me has neither wit
nor wisdom to say the things that I have said.
I can expound on history or science
although I never got beyond eighth grade.
But the whole spirit world is in compliance
with my needs. This isn't a charade.
There is no heaven waiting when you die—
that would be too easy—but your soul
journeys onwards. And such souls supply
me with the answers that you find so droll.
You're welcome. This is what God meant me for.
And don't forget—collection's by the door.

My Life as an Apache Scout

White men are afraid of me. Their wives
simper in long skirts. I ride and fight,
sworn to defend the honor and the lives
of the Apache people. In the night
I sometimes fox walk through their clumsy camp
and listen to their snoring. In the day
I track them clearly by the noisy tramp
as they pass through our woods. They're easy prey.

But they have guns. We steal them where we can—
I taught the chief, my brother, how to shoot.
And they outnumber us. We need a plan
better than raids and ambushes en route.
As for this drink that makes our braves' heads thick,
enough! We've got no chance once we get sick.

My Life as a Saloon Girl

My sister lives near Richmond on a farm,
three children and another on its way.
I wouldn't trade our lives on any day.
She's got gray hair already; I got charm
so even hardened gunslingers disarm
and draw out wads of rolled-up bills to pay
for my champagne (It's water.) I display
my pretty knees, some cleavage. What's the harm?

My job's to make them think I'm having fun.
They treat me like a lady and don't touch.
I have a little pearly-handled gun
tucked in my garter for when they're out of line,
but honestly, it doesn't happen much.
Come let's join in, they're singing *Clementine*.

My Life as a Victorian Streetwalker

It wasn't wot I dreamed of as a kid—
I thought I'd get the factory or the mill—
but ruddy Barry knocked me up, he did,
an' then the baby kept on falling ill.
I share a basement with a girl called Nell,
an' we take turns to go an' earn the rent,
Most of the blokes are ugly or they smell,
though every now an' then you get a gent.
I mostly think about me little boy,
not God or punishment for mortal sin.
'E is the only thing that brings me joy,
an' wot's the point? There's no way I can win.
I'm up against the wall or on me back,
an' either way the next one might be Jack.

My Life as a Missionary in West Africa

I couldn't wait to sail from Edinburgh
and leave the mills of Aberdeen behind.
The voyage, the first few weeks are all a blur—
I was afraid, of course, of what I'd find.
But soon I knew what God had had in mind—
it was my role to challenge superstition
and witchcraft, which they used in every kind.
I fought at length against the cruel tradition
of killing newborn twins on the suspicion
they were conceived by demons. Savage fools!
I saved the babies, brought them to the mission
and set them up in English Bible schools.
For years I worked His magic on that coast
and every night I thanked the Holy Ghost.

My Life as a Can-Can Dancer

There's nothing like it! When we form the line
most men lean forward slightly in their seat
and while we dance, forget to drink their wine
hoping for a glimpse of something sweet.
I flaunt my petticoats and flash my thighs—
high kicks, jump splits—it's meant to be erotic.
They all want us—I see it in their eyes.
The choreography is so hypnotic
they can't do anything but sit and stare
and at the end our skirts fly overhead
so they can see our frilly underwear.
I have my pick of whom I take to bed
letting them know that if they're happy to
they may leave gifts of money. Most men do.

My Life as a Gangster's Moll

I'd been to good schools but I wanted more—
liquor, danger, bad boys, lots of money.
He was handsome, charming, and he swore
we would be rich. The scam we planned was funny—
after I lured this old guy into bed
and posed for snaps, we threatened to tar his name
unless he promptly coughed up loads of bread,
an easy rip-off called the badger game.
I don't know what went wrong—all seemed on plan.
The first installment came through right on time.
Perhaps the bills were marked? Anyway, my man
died in a shoot out with the Feds. Now I'm
under an alias and on the run.
I'm not sure what comes next but jeez it's fun!

My Life as a Polish Nun During World War II

We ran an orphanage in old Gdansk,
which overflowed in nineteen thirty-nine.
Daily, the Germans rolled by in their tanks.
We kept our heads well down and toed the line.
But any child that came here in the night,
no questions asked, was never turned away –
starving, beaten, sick, half-dead with fright,
Christian or Jew—with orphans, who can say?

We had to teach the Jewish ones the creed,
so the Gestapo wouldn't know our game.
The irony of sowing that small seed,
it wasn't lost on me, though not our aim.
Children are dear to God, gentile or Jew.
We wanted to save them all; we saved a few.

My Life in the Jim Crow South

I've always gone to church with Ma and Pa
and liked it fine, but this new preacher man
is different—he's against the Jim Crow law.

Pa keeps saying that the Ku Klux Klan
is gonna whip his ass. But he ain't scared.
He's from the North and got himself a plan.

Preacher says now we all gotta be prepared.
I'm so hoping things will change round here.
He's been getting the old schoolhouse repaired.

I'm gonna learn to read and write next year.
Preacher keeps saying what white folk say is lies.
He's real smart but I still feel the fear

when I gotta walk by them old white guys
and Mister Collins just looks at me with those eyes.

My Life as a Hollywood Madam

I started as a call girl, though not cheap,
but turning tricks was never quite my thing,
so, being good at math I made the leap
to management, and soon I had a ring
of girls in my employ—all classic beauties
fit to grace the arms of influential
bankers and officials. Several cuties
even dallied with the presidential.
I made a mint and stashed it well offshore
and when the Feds came sniffing I smelled sweet.
I also had some, shall we say, *rapport*
in highish places? Still, I felt the heat,
and that's why I retired at forty-two.
What are you drinking? Tell me all about *you.*

My Life in the Order of the Missionaries of Charity

Let's get this straight: the woman was a saint
whether they make her one or not. At twenty
for her I left a world of shallow plenty
and on that count will offer no complaint.

Like her, I followed God's specific call
to help the poorest of the poor, got sent
to one of her Homes for the Dying, whose intent
was to provide a noble death for all.

But "noble death" to her meant something odd—
that everyone should suffer like the Lord
so pleas for drugs to ease pain were ignored
and dying men went screaming unto God.

I couldn't deal with it so I resigned,
citing ill health. The Christ I love is kind.

My Life as a Canadian Dominatrix

It's hard to run my business on the street—
to do it right you need props and a setting.
My brothel had a superb dungeon suite—
perhaps that's what the courts found so upsetting
and yet by striking laws down that were letting
girls like me perform in private places,
safely, comfortably, they were abetting
the seedy trade that poisons public spaces.
I chose to fight, became one of those faces
you see in every tabloid. It's quite strange—
I've learned the law now, studied several cases.
I'd contemplate a mid-life career change
except they're hypocrites. At every turn
I see ex-clients, desperate to adjourn.

My Life as a Transgender Hooker

I almost pass. To men who stink of booze
my breasts seem real, or real as any fake
implants a girl can get. I wear flat shoes,
though soon I'm kneeling anyway. I make
appreciative sounds about their junk.
It's all they need. I keep my own well bound
and don't let them get near it. Sometimes drunk
men grope me there, but even then I've found
that most are titillated at the thought.
Sexual preference isn't as precise
as Christians think. The worst? When I got caught
they stuck me in the men's cells down at Vice.
I'm saving to cross over all the way,
but twenty dollar tricks? Perhaps one day...

My Life as a Crack Whore

Need a hit so bad I'm gonna die.
Pull my skirt up so some guy will stop.
Everything goes away when I get high.

Got raped once and went to see a cop.
Laughed and said he wondered why I cared,
searched me with his hands inside my top.

Get high when I'm hungry, cold or scared.
Miss my kids—they're at my ma's. It's cool.
Haven't seen them lately, haven't dared.

Pipe-dream of quitting, going back to school
be a counselor for drugs, 'cos I
get what it's like. Yeah, I'm no one's fool.

Know you can't stop easy. This is why:
everything goes away when you get high.

My Life as a Tibetan Yogini

The hand that points to the moon is not the moon.
I don't pretend to teach, I meditate
upon the eightfold path, sometimes commune

with other seekers after truth. If fate
be willing I shall reach nirvana yet.
It doesn't matter. I'm prepared to wait

as many lives as those I now forget
that I've already lived. I am content
to be inside the moment, and to let

the universe unfold as she is meant.
I find her frequency and try to tune
it in before my shrine, inhale the scent

of lotus blossom and jasmine as I croon,
The hand that points to the moon is not the moon.

Acknowledgments

Grateful acknowledgment is made to the editors and publishers of the following publications in which these poems first appeared: "My Life as Ghengis Khan's Morganatic Wife" and "My Life as an Anglo-Saxon Novitiate" in *Mezzo Cammin*, "My Life as a Vestal Virgin" and "My Life as a Camp Follower" in *Angle*, "My Life as One of King Charles II's Mistresses" in *Light*, "My Life as a Serving Wench of the Round Table" in *The Rotary Dial*, "My life as a Hollywood Madam" in *E-Verse Radio*. "My Life as a Druidess", "My Life as a French Carmelite Nun", "My Life as a Saloon Girl" and "My Life as a Polish Nun During World War II" in *The Road Not Taken*.

Most of these poems were written during a two-week residency at the Virginia Center for the Creative Arts.

About the Poet

Anna M. Evans' poems have appeared in the *Harvard Review, Atlanta Review, Rattle, American Arts Quarterly,* and *32 Poems.* She gained her MFA from Bennington College, and is the Editor of the *Raintown Review.* Recipient of Fellowships from the MacDowell Artists' Colony and the Virginia Center for the Creative Arts, and winner of the 2012 Rattle Poetry Prize Readers' Choice Award, she currently teaches at West Windsor Art Center and Richard Stockton College of NJ. Her chapbook, *The Stolen From: Poems About Memory & Alzheimer's,* is available from Barefoot Muse Press. Visit her online at www.annamevans.com.

29091767R00031

Made in the USA
Charleston, SC
01 May 2014